Beanie and The Bamboozling Book Machine

A New Fantasy Adventure for Children

by Bob May,
Christopher Tibbetts
and Roy C. Booth

A Samuel French Acting Edition

New York Hollywood London Toronto
SAMUELFRENCH.COM

Copyright © 1990 Bob May

ALL RIGHTS RESERVED

CAUTION: Professionals and amateurs are hereby warned that *BEANIE AND THE BAMBOOZLING BOOK MACHINE* is subject to a Licensing Fee. It is fully protected under the copyright laws of the United States of America, the British Commonwealth, including Canada, and all other countries of the Copyright Union. All rights, including professional, amateur, motion picture, recitation, lecturing, public reading, radio broadcasting, television and the rights of translation into foreign languages are strictly reserved. In its present form the play is dedicated to the reading public only.

The amateur live stage performance rights to *BEANIE AND THE BAMBOOZLING BOOK MACHINE* are controlled exclusively by Samuel French, Inc., and licensing arrangements and performance licenses must be secured well in advance of presentation. PLEASE NOTE that amateur Licensing Fees are set upon application in accordance with your producing circumstances. When applying for a licensing quotation and a performance license please give us the number of performances intended, dates of production, your seating capacity and admission fee. Licensing Fees are payable one week before the opening performance of the play to Samuel French, Inc., at 45 W. 25th Street, New York, NY 10010.

Licensing Fee of the required amount must be paid whether the play is presented for charity or gain and whether or not admission is charged.

Stock licensing fees quoted upon application to Samuel French, Inc.

For all other rights than those stipulated above, apply to: Samuel French, Inc.

Particular emphasis is laid on the question of amateur or professional readings, permission and terms for which must be secured in writing from Samuel French, Inc.

Copying from this book in whole or in part is strictly forbidden by law, and the right of performance is not transferable.

Whenever the play is produced the following notice must appear on all programs, printing and advertising for the play: "Produced by special arrangement with Samuel French, Inc."

Due authorship credit must be given on all programs, printing and advertising for the play.

ISBN 978-0-573-65004-8   Printed in U.S.A.   #4707

No one shall commit or authorize any act or omission by which the copyright of, or the right to copyright, this play may be impaired.

No one shall make any changes in this play for the purpose of production.

Publication of this play does not imply availability for performance. Both amateurs and professionals considering a production are strongly advised in their own interests to apply to Samuel French, Inc., for written permission before starting rehearsals, advertising, or booking a theatre.

No part of this book may be reproduced, stored in a retrieval system, or transmitted in any form, by any means, now known or yet to be invented, including mechanical, electronic, photocopying, recording, videotaping, or otherwise, without the prior written permission of the publisher.

IMPORTANT BILLING AND CREDIT REQUIREMENTS

All producers of BEANIE AND THE BAMBOOZLING BOOK MACHINE *must* give credit to the Author of the Play in all programs distributed in connection with performances of the Play and in all instances in which the title of the Play appears for purposes of advertising, publicizing or otherwise exploiting the Play and/or a production. The name of the Author *must* also appear on a separate line, on which no other name appears, immediately following the title, and *must* appear in size of type not less than fifty percent the size of the title type.

CAUTIONARY NOTE

The text of BEANIE AND THE BAMBOOZLING BOOK MACHINE makes reference to projections of various popular children's book characters. Producers are hereby cautioned that they must make their own pictures of these characters (e.g. they may not use pictures of these characters from popular motion picture adaptions of the stories, or pictures from published books, as these are not the property of the authors of the play, nor does Samuel French, Inc. control rights to these.

In addition: the text of the play makes reference to theme music from various popular (as of publication of the play) children's TV shows. Permission to produce the play does *not* include permission to use this music. If producers of the play wish to use this music, they must procure permission from the producer of the TV show themselves.

The premiere of *Beanie and the Bamboozling Book Machine* was presented by Bob Dryden at Brainerd Community College Theatre in October of 1989 under the direction of Bob May, with sets, lights and costume designs by Dennis Lamberson, under the stage management of Cathie Theis, with the following cast:

MR WRIGHT..........................Kevin Boyles
BEANIE BOREN .... Cristopher Tibbetts
THE QUEEN .... Becke Webster
CANDY.....................................Dawn Boyer
THE WICKED WITCH OF THE WEST
....Rachel Niemeyer
PROFESSOR LIBRUM..............Denny Demm
DOROTHY........................ Nicole Bourassa
GRETEL.........................Jeanne Gullickson
HANSEL ....Pete Etterman
SNOW WHITE................. Melanie Sundberg
DEWIE DECIMAL............... Tom Hazelwood
HEWIE .... Roy C. Booth
LOUIE............................Brian Gulrandson

BEANIE AND THE BAMBOOZLING BOOK MACHINE

SCENE: An elementary school auditorium. On the stage is a podium, a trophy table adorned with trophies, and an enormous object covered with a sheet. BEANIE is seated in a chair next to the podium and behind the podium, MR. WRIGHT, the principal of the school.

AT RISE: As the LIGHTS come up, BEANIE waves to the audience with a big smile. MR. WRIGHT glares at Beanie and then addresses the audience/students.

MR. WRIGHT. Good afternoon, boys and girls, and welcome to the annual science fair. Before we see a demonstration of this year's winning project by Beanie Boren ... I'd like to give you all a progress report on the "Book-it" Reading Program and how our school stands as we go into the final day of the competition. I am pleased to announce that our school is in second place. With an average of twelve books read per student. (*HE starts to applaud.*) Out top reader is Gidget-Mae Brown with a total of twenty-seven books. (*HE starts to applaud again.*) And in last place with a very disappointing showing is Beanie

time. By turning this switch ...(*HE flips another switch to "on" and the MACHINE starts to hum once again.*) ... I activate the solar panels which will draw energy directly from the sun giving the machine the additional power needed to read the books with the same accuracy as with a single book. To prove my point my machine will now read ... (*As HE announces each book HE inserts the book into the slots. The MACHINE hums louder.*) ... Hansel and Gretel, Snow White and The Wizard of Oz.

(*On the video monitor pictures of the three books flash. Then suddenly witches' faces start to appear. At this point the MACHINE explodes.*)

MR. WRIGHT. Beanie! What's going on here?
BEANIE. Ah ... excuse me, ladies and gentlemen ... it appears we have had a slight malfunction ... ah ... if you'll just give me a second ... I'm sure I can fix the problem in no time.

(*HE starts fiddling around with the machine. SMOKE is pouring from the machine. MR. WRIGHT and BEANIE ad-lib through this.*)

MR. WRIGHT. Well, young man ... I hope you're proud of what you've done. Not only have you embarrassed yourself ... and me ... in front of the entire student body ... but it appears that you have also destroyed the school's electrical system. (*HE looks around.*) No, you've blackened out the entire neighborhood. Now take that key out and turn that machine off before you black out the whole town. You'll never be Book-it champion now, Beanie! And it's all because of your ... bamboozling Book Machine.

(*BEANIE bursts into tears, takes the key out of the machine and runs from the auditorium.*)

MR. WRIGHT. Boys and girls ... Moms and dads ... please remain in your seats. I'm sure our crack custodial staff will have the power restored very shortly. Meanwhile I would like to continue with the program by presenting this year's Book-it champion ... Gidget-Mae Brown ... with the first place trophy. Gidget-Mae ... please join me on stage.

(*At this point a THUNDER CLAP is heard and a FLASH POT goes off and the Queen witch from Snow White appears holding a hand mirror. SHE stares into the mirror as SHE speaks.*)

QUEEN. Mirror ... mirror in my hand ... who's the fairest in the ... wait a minute ... where am I? This is not my castle.
MR. WRIGHT. You're not Gidget-Mae ...
QUEEN. And you're not the King.
MR. WRIGHT. No ... I'm the principal.

QUEEN. Snow White must have put you up to this!
MR. WRIGHT. I'm sorry I don't know a Miss White ... I was expecting a Miss Brown.

(At his point another THUNDER CLAP is heard and another FLASH POT goes off as CANDY, the witch from Hansel and Gretel, appears on stage. SHE thinks Mr. Wright and the Queen are Hansel and Gretel.)

CANDY. Brown chocolate ... red licorice ... green gum drops and all the gingerbread you can eat. Nibble, nibble like a mouse ... who is nibbling at my house? Come ... come inside my lovely house ... dear Hansel and Gretel ... my, how you've grown, my dumplings ...

(At this point another THUNDER CLAP is heard and a third FLASH POT goes off as WEST, the Wicked Witch of the West, from The Wizard of Oz appears on stage. SHE mistakes Mr. Wright, Candy and Queen as characters in her story.)

WEST. I'll get you yet ... my pretties and your little dog, too. Wanna play ball ... Scarecrow? *(SHE starts to throw fireballs at Mr. Wright, Candy, and Queen.)*

QUEEN. Who is that crazy witch?
CANDY. Which witch, are you referring to?

MR. WRIGHT. Stop that ... do you want to burn down my school ... stop throwing that fire ... get some water ... water ... someone get some water.

WEST. (*As SHE runs and hides.*) No water ... no water ...

MR. WRIGHT. Who are all of you?

CANDY. (*Looking at Queen.*) You're not Gretel.

QUEEN. Gretel ... who is this Gretel?

CANDY. She's the cute little girl I'm gonna eat ... along with her brother ... I'm the evil witch, Candy, from the book *Hansel and Gretel*.

QUEEN. You're a witch, too? I am the fair witch from *Snow White*! My friends, the few I have, call me Queen.

WEST. Holy Oz! You don't say ... I'm the Wicked Witch of the West ...

MR. WRIGHT. (*Looking at the machine.*) Beanie!

QUEEN. Beanie? That's an odd name for a witch.

CANDY. What book are you from?

MR. WRIGHT. I'm the principal.

CANDY. The principal witch of a book called "Beanie?" I've never heard of it.

WEST. Are you a good witch or a bad witch?

MR. WRIGHT. I'm not a witch at all.

WEST. You don't say that ... Dorothy says that to Glenda ... right after her house lands on my poor sister ... the Wicked Witch of the East ...

you must be the Good Witch of the South. I didn't think she appeared in the book.

MR. WRIGHT. No ... you don't understand ... I'm not from a book.

QUEEN. Don't believe him ... he's a spy ... Snow White has lots of friends within the castle.

MR. WRIGHT. This isn't a castle ... it's a school.

CANDY. A school ... that means there's lots of little boys and girls around to fatten up!!!! (*SHE laughs in a high screachy voice.*)

WEST. Shut up ... both of you. And you too, Principal Beanie! Don't you realize what has happened? This isn't my story ... or yours ... or yours! We aren't in our books any more ... or for that matter ... in Bookworld ... nowhere near Bookworld. This must be Reality!!! (*Referring to Mr. Wright.*) He must be a sorcerer ...

(*CANDY and QUEEN scream and hide behind West.*)

WEST. How did you do this? How did you bring us here?

MR. WRIGHT. I didn't bring you here ... that's what I've been trying to tell you ... Beanie ... Beanie must have done it ... with his bamboozling Book Machine!

ALL THREE WITCHES. Book Machine???

MR. WRIGHT. Brilliant Beanie's stupid science project. He was reading your three books when something went wrong.

CANDY. I'll say ... I was just about to lure Hansel and his cute little sister into my candy cottage.

QUEEN. (*Looking into her hand mirror.*) And my mirror was just about to tell me ... "I and not Snow White ... was the fairest of them all!!!!!" I want to go back.

WEST. And you call yourselves witches ... Can't you see what has happened ... what this means? We're out of our books ... we're free. And that's good ... I don't know about you ... but at the end of my book I melt.

QUEEN. I'm doomed to dance till I drop in some tacky red-hot iron shoes.

CANDY. And I get baked ... in my own oven.

WEST. But as long as we're out here ... our endings can't come true. We can live forever.

CANDY. Let's destroy the machine.

(*CANDY and QUEEN run to the machine.*)

WEST. Don't touch that machine!!!!! How do we know that we won't destroy ourselves if we destroy the machine? Just get the books out.

CANDY. They won't come out.

QUEEN. They're stuck.

WEST. (*To Mr. Wright.*) How do you work this machine?

MR. WRIGHT. I don't know ... only Beanie knows how to operate it and besides you need a key.

WEST. Where's the key?

MR. WRIGHT. Beanie took it with him when he ran out of here crying.
WEST. Then we must find this Beanie!

(*ALL THREE WITCHES start laughing as the LIGHTS fade. Suspense MUSIC bridges the shift into the next scene, a clearing in the forest. In the original production the auditorium scene was played on the fore stage in front of the curtain. The forest was pre-set behind the curtain. The scene shift should not take long. BEANIE enters with a backpack, a canteen and the machine key.*)

BEANIE. Mr. Wright was right ... I mean correct. I really blew it back there. I'm going to run away to a place so far away ... that nobody's ever even heard of books. It sure got dark ... fast. I don't like the dark. Weird things happen in the dark.

(*Suddenly a loud strange NOISE fills the theatre. It is a spaceship landing. It lands and from the spaceship emerges PROFESSOR LIBRUM, the head librarian from Bookworld. LIBRUM is dressed like a Super Hero, complete with the letters BW on his chest and a cape. BEANIE hides.*)

LIBRUM. (*Knowing exactly where Beanie is.*) Are you Beanie Boren?
BEANIE. I am.

LIBRUM. You've caused a great deal of trouble, young man.

BEANIE. I know ... you don't have to remind me.

LIBRUM. Then you already know about the witches?

BEANIE. (*Coming out from his hiding place.*) I know Mr. Wright was pretty angry. He must have sent you after me. You must be a cop.

LIBRUM. Do I look like a cop? The name's Professor Librum ... head librarian of Bookworld and I've never heard of this Mr. Wright. But if we don't act fast, young man ... both your world and mine will never be the same again.

BEANIE. Bookworld?

LIBRUM. Bookworld! A world in a galaxy far, far away from here where all story book characters live.

BEANIE. In a galaxy far, far away?

LIBRUM. Yes ... (*HE sits down to catch his breath.*) I'm a bit parched from my journey ... may I have a drink from your canteen?

BEANIE. Sure. (*HE hands the canteen to Librum.*)

LIBRUM. (*Takes a drink.*) This isn't water.

BEANIE. It's Gatorade. It quenches the thirst faster than water.

LIBRUM. Tasty ...

BEANIE. Did you say something about some witches?

LIBRUM. (*Stands up and his attitude is once again all business.*) Your Book Machine released three evil witches from their books and we have to find a way to put them back again.

BEANIE. I don't get it.

LIBRUM. Your machine draws its power from the sun, right?

BEANIE. Only when using the Handy-Dandy-Super-Duper-Deluxe-Solar Convertor.

LIBRUM. Which you were using today.

BEANIE. To read The Wizard of ...

LIBRUM. I know what you were reading ...'cause those are the three witches that've escaped.

BEANIE. My machine did all this?

LIBRUM. When all three witches were united in your machine ... their combined powers ... along with the sun's power ... gave them enough energy to escape from their books. That's why it is so dark ... the witches have drained the sun of its brightness. And it will remain this dark until we can put the evil witches back into their books.

BEANIE. I can't do anything. The machine is broken.

LIBRUM. It's not broken ... the power surge of the sun's rays only caused it to overload. We have to get back to the machine ... turn it on ... Do you have the key?

BEANIE. Right here.

LIBRUM. ... and take the books out.

BEANIE. Then they'll go back to their stories?

LIBRUM. No ... but without the books united in your machine ... the witches will be less powerful and they won't be benefiting from the

sun's energy. Then we'll have a fighting chance of getting them back into their books.
BEANIE. How do we do that?
LIBRUM. One thing at a time, sonny. Now let's get going. We must hurry.
BEANIE. Why?
LIBRUM. Because if I know those witches ... and I do ... the machine confuses them ...
BEANIE. That's good.
LIBRUM. No, that's bad ... because it confuses them, they'll be looking for you. And I'll bet they've already started. Now, let's go ... we can take my space rider.

(*Just as BEANIE and LIBRUM are about to climb into the space rider, ALL THREE WITCHES appear and block their way. LIBRUM puts himself between Beanie and the witches.*)

WEST. Not so fast ... my pretties.
QUEEN. But I'm the fairest of them all ...
WEST. If we don't get the key from the kid ... and gain control of the machine ... it won't matter how pretty you are ... you'll end up back in your story doing your dance of doom forever. (*To Librum.*) I'm right. Aren't I, Professor?
LIBRUM. Hello, Miss West.
WEST. Call me Mae ... (*Pause.*) I am right, aren't I?

(*No response from Librum.*)

WEST. Of course I'm right ... otherwise you'd have never left your precious little Bookworld and come down here to help these mortals. I want that key!!!
CANDY. The kid has it around his scrawny little neck.
WEST. Let's get it, Girls!

(*The THREE WITCHES advance as LIBRUM and BEANIE retreat.*)

QUEEN. Give us that key.
LIBRUM. Stand back.
CANDY. The key, little boy!
WEST. I want that key.
LIBRUM. Stand back or you'll regret it.
WEST. Don't make me laugh, Professor. You know your powers are useless outside of Bookworld. (*To the other witches.*) I can handle this by myself. (*SHE advances on Librum and Beanie.*)
LIBRUM. I'm warning you ...
WEST. (*As SHE laughs triumphantly.*) You don't scare me.
LIBRUM. (*As HE takes the canteen from around Beanie's neck and threatens West with it.*) No ... But this does ...
WEST. What's in there?
LIBRUM. Wouldn't you like to know?
WEST. Water?
LIBRUM. One step further and you'll find out.
QUEEN. He's bluffing.

WEST. (*As SHE backs away from Librum.*) I'm not gonna be the one to find out ... water and I don't mix. Candy, go get the key.
CANDY. I'm not going near that brat ... how do I know water doesn't have the same effect on all witches?
WEST. Was it written into your story?
CANDY. How should I know? ... I can't read.
WEST. I'm surrounded by idiots. Believe me, you two are safe from water ... now cover me and let's get that key.

(*CANDY and QUEEN stand in front of WEST and THEY all advance on Librum and Beanie.*)

WEST. Give me that key.

(*LIBRUM tosses the contents of the canteen on the witches. THEY back off screaming.*)

LIBRUM. Run Beanie ... Get out of here ... Run ...

(*BEANIE and LIBRUM exit through the audience.*)

WEST. I'm melting ... I'm melting!!!
QUEEN. No you're not.
CANDY. You're fine ... a little wet but fine.
WEST. What is this stuff?
QUEEN. I don't know.
CANDY. (*Smelling and tasting.*) It's Gatorade.

QUEEN. It does wonders for alligator skin!!!
WEST. Shut up ... They've escaped!!! They're probably on their way back to the machine. We must get there before they do. Let's go.

(*The stage LIGHTS fade as the WITCHES run into the audience. HOUSE LIGHTS up a bit. As the WITCHES go up the aisles THEY ask the children, "Where did they go? Which way?" etc. The scene is being shifted back to the school auditorium. As soon as the shift is completed the WITCHES exit, HOUSE LIGHTS out, STAGE LIGHTS up and BEANIE and LIBRUM enter.*)

BEANIE. (*Referring to the machine.*) It's over here ... Now all we have to do is take the books out?
LIBRUM. And that will lessen their power.

(*THEY start walking to the machine but MR. WRIGHT steps out and blocks their way. HE is carrying a yard stick as a weapon.*)

MR. WRIGHT. Halt ... who goes there?
BEANIE. It's me, Beanie ...
MR. WRIGHT. Beanie who?
LIBRUM. How many Beanies do you know? (*To Beanie.*) Who is this fool?
BEANIE. The principal of our school.

BEANIE AND THE ... BOOK MACHINE 23

LIBRUM. I can see why you're only a prince and not a king. Put down that ridiculous weapon and let the boy through to his machine.

MR. WRIGHT. This boy's caused enough problems with that bamboozling machine. Who do you think you are?

LIBRUM. I, sir Prince, am Professor Librum, summa cum laude, head librarian of Bookworld ... and I have come to save your planet ... now stand aside and let the boy through!!!!

MR. WRIGHT. (*As HE steps aside.*) Well, why didn't you say so sooner?

LIBRUM. Hurry, Beanie ... we must pull those books out.

(*BEANIE runs to the machine, but CANDY appears and blocks his way.*)

CANDY. Going some place ... Give me that key ... my little weenie.

BEANIE. That's Beanie, ma'am. (*HE turns and throws the key to Librum.*) Catch, Professor.

LIBRUM. (*Catching the key.*) Beautiful throw, Beanie.

QUEEN. (*Appears behind Librum.*) But not as beautiful as I. Now give me that key, Professor.

(*QUEEN starts to cast a spell over Librum, but HE manages to turn and throw the key to WRIGHT.*)

LIBRUM. Catch ... Prince!

WEST. (*Appears in front of Wright and SHE catches the key.*) Nice toss, Professor. Now the key is mine. (*To Beanie.*) Get away from that machine, Beanie.

(*BEANIE runs to Librum.*)

LIBRUM. Why do you want that key? The machine is broken.
WEST. I want to get the books out.
LIBRUM. Why?
WEST. So we can live forever and the world will be ours.
LIBRUM. If you take the books out ... you'll die.
BEANIE. I thought you said it would only decrease their powers.
LIBRUM. SHHHH!!!!! (*To West.*) We have to fix the machine. Don't take the books out.
WEST. I don't believe you, Professor. (*Throwing the key to Candy.*) Turn it on and take the books out.
CANDY. (*Turns to the machine, hesitates and says:*) What if he's telling the truth? Maybe we should leave the books in.
WEST. He's bluffing again. Just like ... with the water. He doesn't want us to take the books out. We won't die. Take them out. (*To Librum.*) Aren't you going to try and stop us?
LIBRUM. You hold the key to success. Take the books out if you must.
WEST. Proceed, my dear Candy.

(*CANDY puts the key in the machine and turns it on. The machine LIGHTS UP and begins to hum. CANDY begins to pull the books out. BEANIE and LIBRUM have their fingers crossed; as CANDY starts to pull the second book out all THREE WITCHES start falling to the floor.*)

WEST. (*Screaming.*) STOP!!! I'm growing weaker ... Put the book back in. Hurry ... hurry ... My power is draining fast ... Quick !!!!!
QUEEN. Yes, hurry .... My beauty is fading...

(*CANDY is struggling to get up and put the books back in the machine. Can she do it? Yes ... SHE does. SHE turns off the machine.*)

WEST. (*Backing LIBRUM, BEANIE and WRIGHT up against the machine.*) You tried to trick me. You wanted us to take the books out. That's not very nice. (*To Candy.*) Take the key out and destroy it.

(*CANDY breaks the key in half.*)

WEST. Bring the boy to me.

(*CANDY drags Beanie to West.*)

WEST. You, my little pretty ... will be my prisoner for the rest of your miserable life ... and without you or a key to your machine ... it will gather dust for eternity. And you can never send us back.

MR. WRIGHT. You'll never get away with this in my school.

WEST. Silence!!! Candy ... cast a spell over those two.

QUEEN. She got to break the key ... Let me do it.

WEST. Fine ... just get it over with.

QUEEN. Let's see now ... which one shall I do??? Oh .. that's a good one! Nooooooo! How about ... well ... Oh, yes, that one is a splendid one ...

WEST. Just do it!!!

QUEEN. (*Looking into her hand mirror.*) Mirror, mirror in my hand ... make them freeze right where they stand.

(*SHE turns the mirror on Librum and Wright. The LIGHTS flash and we hear a spell SOUND. LIBRUM and WRIGHT freeze.*)

WEST. Now for our own safety we better split up ... each of us go our separate ways. I'll take the boy.

CANDY. Why do you get the boy? I can take care of him.

WEST. Enough ... begone ...

BEANIE AND THE ... BOOK MACHINE 27

(*With a THUNDER CLAP and a FLASH POT, SHE disappears with BEANIE.*)

QUEEN. That was rude ... and after I've done some of my best work.
CANDY. Forget her ... come with me to the forest ... I'll build us a nice gingerbread house and soon all the little kiddies will be gnawing at our door.

(*With a THUNDER CLAP and FLASH THEY are gone. After a moment LIBRUM breaks his freeze and runs to check if the witches are truly gone. Seeing that they are HE turns back to Wright waves his hands around Wright's head, a spell SOUND EFFECT is heard, and WRIGHT wakes up from his freeze.*)

MR. WRIGHT. How did you do that?
LIBRUM. Her spell didn't affect me ... I have some powers that work down here. (*HE pulls out a communicator, presses some buttons and then speaks into it.*) Kirk to transporter room. (*HE turns to Wright and laughs.*) I've always wanted to say that. (*Back to the communicator.*) Librum to transporter room.
VOICE. (*Voice over.*) What do you want, Professor?
LIBRUM. Beam down the primary characters from the following books: *Hansel and Gretel*, *Snow White*, and *The Wizard of Oz*.
VOICE. (*Voice over.*) Will that be all, sir?

28   BEANIE AND THE ... BOOK MACHINE

LIBRUM. Yes ... and do it at once.

(*The LIGHTS start to flicker and the following characters are beamed onto the auditorium stage: DOROTHY, HANSEL, SNOW WHITE, GRETEL and THE THREE DECIMALS. As soon as they are beamed in THEY all surround Librum, all talking at once, asking, "What is going on?" etc.*)

LIBRUM. Silence ...
MR. WRIGHT. And I thought *Star Trek* was just make-believe.
LIBRUM. Mr. Wright, allow me to introduce you to my subjects.

(*As LIBRUM introduces each person SHE/HE steps forward and shakes WRIGHT's hand.*)

LIBRUM. This is Dorothy.
DOROTHY. From *The Wizard of Oz*.
LIBRUM. Gretel.
GRETEL. And my dear Bruder!
HANSEL. Hansel.
LIBRUM. From the book with the same title.

(*SNOW WHITE steps forward and shakes WRIGHT'S hand.*)

MR. WRIGHT. And you must be Snow White.
SNOW WHITE. The pleasure is mine.

(*A PERSON with a gold face and blue lips and blue rings around his eyes, dressed in a gold lamé jumpsuit steps forward.*)

LIBRUM. And this is Dewie Decimal .. you know him ... he invented the Dewie Decimal System ...

(*Another PERSON looking the same steps forward.*)

LIBRUM. And his brother Hewie ...

(*HEWIE shakes WRIGHT's hand.*)

MR. WRIGHT. Hewie!
LIBRUM. ... And Louie.

(*LOUIE shakes WRIGHT's hand.*)

MR. WRIGHT. Louie!
LIBRUM. My assistants in Bookworld!
MR. WRIGHT. Meeting you all is my childhood fantasy come true. (*To Librum.*) But what are they doing here?
LIBRUM. To help ... I know how we can deal with the witches and save Beanie at the same time. We can't put them back into their books ... without a key ... the machine is truly broken .... so we have to fight them the only way we know how. We force each one of them to reenact the

ending of her own story. They meet their fate. That's the only way to end their reign of terror and return things to normal. They're just too powerful to destroy any other way.

GRETEL. We're certainly familiar with the endings of our stories.

LIBRUM. (*As HE places a hand on Gretel's shoulder.*) But you must remember ... this is no longer just a story or a fantasy ... This is for keeps. (*To everyone.*) Everyone ... Line up!!!

(*EVERYONE jumps to attention in a line. WRIGHT after some hesitation joins them in line.*)

LIBRUM. Your mission, should you choose to accept it ...

(*The theme from "Mission Impossible"* plays under the following.*)

LIBRUM. ... is much more dangerous than what you are accustomed to. Your books were predestined to come out a certain way, real life may not be so kind. Everyone who's with me, cross this line.

(*HE draws a line on the stage floor. The DECIMALS don't hesitate at all, THEY step over the line in unison. HANSEL and*

---

* See cautionary note in front matter.

GRETEL look at each other and THEY step over the line. SNOW WHITE and DOROTHY then decide to step over the line. WRIGHT is left behind the line. MUSIC fades out.)

GRETEL. Aren't you going to help, Mr. Wright?

MR. WRIGHT. (*As HE steps over the line.*) Of course ... I just thought I'd let you children go first ... to make sure you made it safely.

LIBRUM. Thank you all for joining me in this crusade against the evil witches. With valiance, determination and teamwork we can rescue Beanie from the clutches of darkness, restore the brilliance to the earth's sun, and send the witches to their fate.

MR. WRIGHT. How do we do that? I suppose with fancy laser guns and spaceships? I bet the *National Enquirer* would love this.

DOROTHY. Mr. Wright ... back on the farm Uncle Henry told us that we all had to work together ... and that's what we have to do now to succeed.

HANSEL. Yes, working together is what saves Gretel and me from the clutches of Candy.

GRETEL. Ja, der Bruder.

MR. WRIGHT. All right ... all right. I'm with you ... I'm with you... But how do we reenact these endings without all the characters here?

LIBRUM. Decimals report.

DEWIE. (*Does a military step forward.*) Snow White character status: The Seven Dwarfs are on strike and wouldn't come. The Prince is fighting with his brother, the Prince from Sleeping Beauty, over who is the better kisser. (*HE steps back.*)

HEWIE. (*Steps forward.*) Hansel and Gretel character status: All primary characters present and accounted for. (*HE steps back.*)

LOUIE. (*Steps forward.*) Report from Oz: The Lion, Scarecrow and Tin Man are caught somewhere within Wonderland and the White Rabbit's not talking. (*HE steps back and then steps forward again.*) And Toto too! (*HE steps back.*).

DEWIE. You know as well as I that Bookworld is a terrible mess because of that machine.

LIBRUM. We'll make due with who we have.

SNOW WHITE. What's next?

DOROTHY. Who's first?

LIBRUM. I think we should start with the Queen. She's vain and will be the easiest to lure back to the school. As soon as she finds out Snow White is here she'll arrive in no time with apple in hand.

SNOW WHITE. How will she know I'm here?

LIBRUM. I'm sure her mirror is telling her now.

HANSEL. But don't we need the Seven Dwarfs to make the reenactment real?

GRETEL. Ja, der Bruder.

LIBRUM. How many people do we have here?

DOROTHY. Eight ... if you don't count Snow White.

LIBRUM. Seven ... I can't help you. They know me too well. You seven will have to play the dwarfs.

MR. WRIGHT. Hey ... our third grade class just finished putting on *Snow White* and I'm sure we still have the costumes. Will that help?

LIBRUM. Ideal! You take everyone and get them dressed, then all report back here.

MR. WRIGHT. Follow me.

(*ALL but SNOW WHITE and LIBRUM exit.*)

SNOW WHITE. I'm scared. I'm really scared.

LIBRUM. There's nothing to be frightened of, my dear.

SNOW WHITE. But I have to eat a poisoned apple.

LIBRUM. I know. And since this is real, who knows what she's done to the apple? It could be full of a stronger poison.

SNOW WHITE. Then I'll only pretend to take a bite.

LIBRUM. No. It has to be real. She'll know if you're faking it and not really asleep.

SNOW WHITE. How will I wake up? The Prince isn't here.

LIBRUM. I promise you ... I will find you a prince to kiss you.

SNOW WHITE. I'm placing my life in your hands, Professor.

LIBRUM. You're a true beauty.

(*THEY embrace, and SNOW WHITE remembers:*)

SNOW WHITE. But what about the red-hot iron shoes? The Queen has to dance in the shoes.
LIBRUM. I'll send one of the Decimals back to Bookworld for them. Don't worry, Snow White.
SNOW WHITE. I trust you.

(*The OTHERS enter dressed as Dwarfs. The costumes are too small for everyone. Remember, they were made for Wright's third grade class.*)

SNOW WHITE. (*Upon seeing them.*) This isn't going to work.
LIBRUM. Trust me. (*To the Dwarfs.*) Now, to speed things along ... you Dwarfs go through the neighborhood and spread the word that Snow White is at the school, and she—not the Queen—is the fairest of them all.

(*The SEVEN DWARFS walk through the audience spreading the word. THEY exit at the back of the theatre.*)

LIBRUM. You must act normal. (*Remembering.*) What is it you do in your story?
SNOW WHITE. Well ... I cooked and cleaned for the Dwarfs.

LIBRUM. Okay ... start cleaning the stage.

(*SNOW WHITE gets a broom and starts to sweep the stage.*)

LIBRUM. I can't just sit here. It'll probably take the Queen awhile to get the word ... To save time, I'll take my space rider back to Bookworld to get the red-hot iron shoes.
SNOW WHITE. Do you have to leave me? Can't you send one of the Decimals? Like you said.
LIBRUM. Time is the of the essence, my child.

(*LIBRUM kisses her goodbye, and exits for Bookworld. The space rider is heard taking off. SNOW WHITE waves goodbye, then starts to hum happily and rearrange the furniture. SHE puts the trophy table center stage. The QUEEN enters, disguised as an old hag, carrying a basket of apples.*)

QUEEN. Snow White?
SNOW WHITE. Yes.
QUEEN. Librum sent me from Bookworld.
SNOW WHITE. Who are you?
QUEEN. I'm the Old Woman who lived in a shoe. He's worried about you so he sent me to look after you.
SNOW WHITE. Oh, how nice.
QUEEN. Always thinking, that man.

SNOW WHITE. Tell me ... I've always wondered ... how did you ever manage to keep track of all those kids?

QUEEN. It was a small shoe. (*SHE laughs at her joke.*) And they always knew if they misbehaved that they wouldn't eat that night.

SNOW WHITE. Oh food! I am so hungry. I haven't had a bite to eat since that crazy machine sent Bookworld upside down.

QUEEN. Well, I have an apple. (*SHE offers Snow White an apple.*)

SNOW WHITE. An apple? I don't think so ...

QUEEN. Oh that's right ... How silly of me ... apples and you don't get along. (*SHE laughs.*) So ... how's it going? Do you know where the witches are?

SNOW WHITE. No, but we have a plan.

QUEEN. That's good. Can you tell me about it?

SNOW WHITE. Well, Librum thinks if we ... maybe I will have that apple after all.

QUEEN. Take your pick.

(*The QUEEN holds out the basket of apples. SNOW WHITE selects one and is about to take a bite when LIBRUM enters on the run and shouts:*)

LIBRUM. Don't eat that ...

(*It is too late. SNOW WHITE has taken a bite and falls to the floor, asleep.*)

QUEEN. Apple? (*SHE begins to dance triumphantly.*) I've won! I've won, Professor ... I've won. Now I'm the fairest of them all ... Not Snow White. I've won ... I've won.

(*SHE dances offstage laughing. The Seven Dwarfs enter at the back of the house. THEY see Snow White and run screaming through the audience to the stage.*)

HEWIE. (*To Librum.*) What happened, boss?

(*During the following dialogue LOUIE and HANSEL lay SNOW WHITE on the trophy table.*)

LIBRUM. I only left her for a moment.
DEWIE. What for?
LIBRUM. To get the red-hot iron dancing shoes.

(*The QUEEN laughs offstage.*)

MR. WRIGHT. Well, you've made a mess of this.
HEWIE. Where are they?
LIBRUM. I couldn't find them. Bookworld is crazier now than when we left it.

(*The QUEEN laughs offstage.*)

GRETEL. What do we do now?

MR. WRIGHT. (*Referring to the Queen offstage.*) She's dancing over there now. Won't that seal her doom?

LOUIE. Not without the magic shoes.

HEWIE. Without the magic shoes ... she can dance forever and the only thing that will happen is ... she'll get tired.

LIBRUM. I'm afraid we've lost.

(*The QUEEN laughs offstage. Pause. ALL are depressed. THEY have lost. Then suddenly DOROTHY steps forward with a ray of hope and says:*)

DOROTHY. What about my magic slippers? Glenda told me there were very powerful.

LIBRUM. Only in Oz!

GRETEL. It's worth a try ... for Snow White's sake.

LIBRUM. She's right.

DOROTHY. (*Takes off her slippers, holds them out and taps them together.*) Make her dance 'til she drops.

(*A spell SOUND EFFECT is heard. The QUEEN enters laughing.*)

QUEEN. I've won ... I've won ...

LIBRUM. Yes ... you've won, my Queen. You are the fairest of them all. (*HE bows to her.*) May I have this dance?

QUEEN. Oh, my feet are killing me.
DOROTHY. Try my slippers, oh, beautiful Queen. In Oz they are magical. They'll make your feet feel better. (*SHE hands her slippers to the Queen.*)
QUEEN. Well, thank you. (*SHE puts the shoes on.*) Oh, yes ... they are wonderful ... my feet feel heavenly. Professor, I would love to dance.
LIBRUM. You don't need me as a partner.
QUEEN. What do you mean?
DOROTHY. Dance, shoes.

(*SHE claps her hands together. Eerie SOUNDS fill the theatre as the QUEEN starts to dance wildly around the stage. After a moment HEWIE and LOUIE carry the screaming QUEEN off. ALL others ad-lib in celebration as THEY surround Librum. HEWIE and LOUIE enter and join the celebration.*)

MR. WRIGHT. One down, two to go.
HANSEL. Can we take care of Candy next?
GRETEL. But we don't know where she is, der Bruder.
DEWIE. I do ... While I was out spreading the word about Snow White I discovered the location of her new gingerbread house. It's in a clearing in the forest ... not very far from here.
HANSEL. Let's go get her!
LIBRUM. Not so fast, my brave little Hansel.
HANSEL. What's the matter?

LIBRUM. You must calm down and go into this with your eyes open.
DOROTHY. Look what happened to Snow White.
HANSEL. Why? We have all of you to protect us.
LIBRUM. No. To make the story as real as possible, you two must face Candy alone. We will be close by ... but you and Gretel are on your own. Come, you must change, and we'll all go to the edge of the forest with you.

(*ALL exit except DOROTHY and LIBRUM.*)

DOROTHY. What about Snow White?
LIBRUM. She's safe as long as she sleeps.

(*LIBRUM puts his arm around Dorothy and THEY exit. The LIGHTS fade as we hear "The Mod Squad"* TV show theme. The CURTAIN closes to set the stage for Candy's gingerbread cottage and oven in the forest. In front of the curtain WEST and BEANIE are down left in a LIGHT special. WEST is looking in her crystal ball. SHE holds Beanie with a spiked leash around his neck. The MUSIC fades.*)

WEST. So ... they've managed to do away with the Queen. Now they're on their way to

---

* See cautionary note in front matter.

Candy. I'll wait to see how they fare there before I deal with you, young man.

BEANIE. Why are you so wicked?

WEST. I'm a witch. It's my job.

BEANIE. I'm so stupid. If I'd only read those books ...

WEST. You're not so stupid, you freed me with your machine.

BEANIE. You won't be free for long. My friends will take care of you.

WEST. Dream on, sprout. (*SHE looks into the crystal ball.*) Oh, I see they're at the edge of the forest.

(*The LIGHTS fade. We hear the theme to "The Wild Wild West"* TV show. The CURTAIN opens and the scene is Candy's gingerbread cottage and oven in the forest. CANDY comes out of her cottage. The MUSIC fades.*)

CANDY. (*Admiring her cottage.*) It's beautiful. My gingerbread cottage is completed ... and just in time for dinner. Now where's that vain Queen? She said she'd be right back. And something about Snow White at the school. That's impossible. And she took my apples. I was going to make caramel apples out of them. Wait a minute ... if Snow White is here and not in Bookworld, maybe Hansel and Gretel are here

---

* See cautionary note in front matter.

too. I'd better be aware of all children. One can never be too careful.

(*SHE exits laughing into her cottage. The OTHERS sneak in.*)

DEWIE. There it is.
LIBRUM. (*To Hansel and Gretel.*) Play your scene, and play it well. You must push Candy into the oven. (*To the others.*) Everyone else ... surround the house ... And keep out of sight.
MR. WRIGHT. We're behind you all the way, kids.
DOROTHY. Don't be scared, Gretel.

(*ALL except HANSEL and GRETEL hide.*)

HANSEL. Are you ready, sister?
GRETEL. Ja, der Bruder.

(*THEY both take a deep breath, cross to the cottage and begin to eat pieces of the house. CANDY comes out.*)

CANDY. Nibble, nibble, like a mouse, who is nibbling at my house?
GRETEL. We're hungry and we're lost.
CANDY. Well, my nice young children eat all you want ... there's plenty of sweets for everyone. (*SHE then realizes.*) Wait! You're Hansel and Gretel! Get away from here! You're not welcome!

HANSEL. No ... we're not ... them. We're ... ahh ... ahh ...

GRETEL. He's Little Boy Blue and I'm Little Bo Peep. And I've lost my sheep and I don't know where to find them. (*SHE begins to cry.*)

CANDY. Well I haven't seen any sheep.

GRETEL. Perhaps they're hiding over there in that oven. (*SHE cries louder.*)

CANDY. That's ridiculous.

GRETEL. Are you sure? (*SHE continues to cry.*)

HANSEL. Don't cry, Little Bo Beep. We'll find your sheep.

GRETEL. I know they're in that oven. (*Big cry.*)

CANDY. (*SHE can no longer take the crying.*) They are not. I'll show you.

(*CANDY walks to the oven. HANSEL and GRETEL hang back. THEY are pleased that getting Candy to the oven has been so easy. CANDY opens the oven door, HANSEL and GRETEL run to push her in, but CANDY quickly turns on them.*)

CANDY. Oh no you don't. Thought you could fool me. Little Bo Peep, my foot. You're Hansel and Gretel. I'll take care of you. (*SHE raises her arms and casts a spell over them.*) Gumdrops, bubble gum, jellybeans ... red, green and blue. Away from my cottage ... Begone with you.

(*A weird SOUND fills the theatre as HANSEL and GRETEL spin down right. A STROBE LIGHT should be used here for the full effect. CANDY laughs and goes into her cottage. The OTHERS gather around Hansel and Gretel. THEY are hiding behind a rock.*)

HANSEL. It's no use, Professor ... Candy's too clever for us down here.
GRETEL. Ja, der Bruder.
LIBRUM. We can't give up so easily.
MR. WRIGHT. But what can we do?
LIBRUM. They must try again.
DOROTHY. Yes, Auntie Em always said, if at first you don't succeed, try, try, again.
LIBRUM. Your Auntie Em is right. She's a very smart woman.
HANSEL. Then we'll try again.
GRETEL. Ja, der Bruder.
HEWIE. Perhaps they should disguise themselves.
LIBRUM. An excellent idea!
HEWIE. Maybe they could be Little Red Riding Hood and the Big Bad Wolf.
DEWIE. The Fisherman and this Wife.
LOUIE. Beauty and the Beast.
HANSEL. How about Jack and Jill?
GRETEL. Ja, der Bruder.
LIBRUM. Hansel put this band-aid on your forehead.

BEANIE AND THE ... BOOK MACHINE 45

(*HE gives Hansel a band-aid. HANSEL puts it on his forehead.*)

LIBRUM. And Gretel take this pail. (*HE hands Gretel a small pail.*)

LIBRUM. Good luck. You must succeed. Every moment the witches are out of their books they are gaining strength. (*To the others.*) Everyone else ... Back to your hiding places.

(*ALL hide except HANSEL and GRETEL. With a look to each other, HANSEL and GRETEL run to the cottage yelling, "Help help!!!" CANDY comes out of the cottage.*)

CANDY. What's the matter? (*Seeing them.*) Who are you? Hansel and Gretel?
GRETEL. Jack and Jill! My name is Jill, and this is my Bruder ... Jack!
HANSEL. Yes! Yes, I'm Jack, and this is my sister, Jill.
GRETEL. Ja, der Bruder ... I mean, Bro.

(*THEY give each other a "high five."*)

CANDY. Very well ... What's all this hollering about?
GRETEL. We were on our way up the hill to fetch a pail of water.
HANSEL. I fell down and broke my crown.
GRETEL. And I came tumbling after.

HANSEL. Jill skinned her knee and we were wondering if you might have another band-aid?

CANDY. What does this look like? A hospital? (*SHE waves her hands above Hansel and Gretel's heads putting THEM in a trance. Then talks to herself.*) A band-aid? You don't fool me. I know who you are. You want to play games? I should throw you both in the oven right now. But I feel so powerful. I'll play your games, with you awake and you'll soon be my dinner cooking in my oven. (*SHE waves her hands over their heads again bringing THEM out of the trance. SHE talks to them.*) I haven't any band-aids, but how about a nice, juicy gingerbread man? That'll make you feel better.

HANSEL. No, thank you ... but they do look delicious. How do you make them?

CANDY. In my own special oven. I'm cooking a batch right now, would you like to see it?

HANSEL and GRETEL. Oh yes, please.

CANDY. Right this way. (*SHE leads them over to the oven.*) I cook lots of sweet things inside my oven. (*SHE opens the door of the oven.*)

HANSEL. (*Whispering to Gretel.*) Do it now.

CANDY. (*Turning very quickly.*) What was that?

HANSEL. Ahh ... I ... uh ...

GRETEL. Are you cooking something now? ... he said.

BEANIE AND THE ... BOOK MACHINE

CANDY. I've already told you. Nice, juicy gingerbread men. Reach into the back and get one.
HANSEL. No thank you, we've been told never to take food from strangers.
CANDY. But I'm not a stranger. I know who you are ...
GRETEL. (*Yelling and this catches Candy off guard.*) Oh my goodness ... What's that?
CANDY. What? Where?
HANSEL. In the oven.
CANDY. I don't see anything.
GRETEL. Look closer. Way inside.
CANDY. (*Looks inside the oven.*) Where?
HANSEL and GRETEL. RIGHT THERE!

(*THEY push Candy into the oven and slam the doors closed.*)

HANSEL. We did it, sister. We did it.
GRETEL. Ja, der Bruder!

(*EVERYONE emerges from their hiding place, shouting congratulations.*)

MR. WRIGHT. Two down, one to go!
LIBRUM. The toughest one of all.
DOROTHY. But where is she?
LIBRUM. Ahh, that's the question my dear. Does anyone know?
HEWIE. I don't.
LOUIE. Me neither.

DOROTHY. We'll never find her. She's too smart for us.

MR. WRIGHT. Hold on! You mean to say that eight brilliant brains are going to be outdone by one wicked witch?

LIBRUM. He's right. Let's put our heads together.

GRETEL. Dorothy, you know her better than any of us. Tell us something about her.

MR. WRIGHT. I know ... I know! She's afraid of water!

DOROTHY. He's right!

DEWIE. So where would a person go if they were afraid of water?

GRETEL. Someplace high.

HANSEL. Someplace dry.

HEWIE. The mountains!

LIBRUM. NO ... The desert!

(The theme from "The Mod Squad"* TV show plays as THEY all run off and the LIGHTS FADE. The CURTAIN closes and the set is shifted to West's castle as the following two scenes are played in front of the curtain. WEST and BEANIE are discovered down left in the special LIGHT. WEST is looking into her crystal ball. BEANIE still has the collar around his neck. The MUSIC fades as the LIGHTS come up.)

---

* See cautionary note in front matter.

WEST. So! They've figured out where I am, but by the time they get here, you won't be alive ... I figure it will take them one day to get here, but you've only got ... (*SHE turns over an hourglass.*) ... one hour

BEANIE. What if I told you I could fix the machine?

WEST. But the key is broken.

BEANIE. It doesn't matter. I can fix the machine. We could bring in reinforcements ... Think of it. The machine could bring the witches from *Rapunzel* and *Sleeping Beauty*. They could help you. The witch from Sleeping Beauty could surround your castle with brambles. No one could ever reach you then.

WEST. Can you really do this?

BEANIE. Yes! Trust me! Just give me a chance!

WEST. (*Hesitates, then shakes her head.*) NO! You're trying to trick me! I'll deal with your foolish friends all by myself. I'm just sorry you won't be around to see it, Boney.

BEANIE. That's Beanie, ma'am.

(*As the LIGHTS fade the theme from "Inspector Gadget"* TV show plays, minus the vocal. ALL enter from the back of the audience. This time THEY are dressed for the Wizard of Oz. The DECIMALS are dressed as the palace guards, HANSEL is the Tin Man, GRETEL is*

---

* See cautionary note in front matter.

the Scarecrow, and WRIGHT is the Cowardly Lion. DOROTHY is herself. THEY sneak through the audience to the stage, down right. EVERYONE gathers around LIBRUM. The MUSIC fades.)

DOROTHY. Thanks to your space rider, Professor, we got here in fifty-two minutes.
MR. WRIGHT. Forty-five minutes, Dorothy. Your watch must be fast.
DOROTHY. Oh, you're correct, Mr. Wright. (*Pause.*) I'm so nervous ...
HANSEL. These costumes are great.
GRETEL. We're lucky, Mr. Wright, your fourth grade class presented *The Wizard of Oz* last year.
DOROTHY. Now that we're here, what do we do?
LIBRUM. Act out the story just like it's written. You Decimals, mix in with the other guards, and when these four get to the gate, let them in. (*HE points to Dorothy, Hansel, Gretel and Wright. The DECIMALS shake their heads affirmative and exit.*)
DOROTHY. Aren't you coming?
LIBRUM. I can't. The Wicked Witch will sense my presence. Good luck, and may the powers of Bookworld be with you.

(THEY all huddle and begin to hum. The CURTAIN opens to reveal West's castle under BLACK LIGHT. There are many fluorescent

skulls painted on the set that the black light reflects. Led by the SCARECROW/GRETEL, ALL but LIBRUM make a circle of the stage looking for Beanie. LIBRUM has exited. Suspense MUSIC underscores the search. BEANIE is discovered in a small cage and the MUSIC fades, the BLACK LIGHT goes out, and stage LIGHTS come up.)

BEANIE. I KNEW you would all make it before the hour was up.
HANSEL. Where's the Wicked Witch?
BEANIE. I'm not sure, she just left a minute ago.
MR. WRIGHT. We haven't got much time. Get him out.
HANSEL. How?
GRETEL. He's skinny enough. Let him crawl through the bars.

(BEANIE climbs through the bars of the cage. At that moment, WEST enters with the THREE DECIMALS still dressed as her palace guards.)

WEST. Welcome to my castle. (*To the Guards.*) Seize them!

(A small chase begins, ending with DEWIE catching HANSEL and LOUIE catching WRIGHT and HEWIE catching GRETEL. BEANIE and DOROTHY stand UC. WEST walks down the castle steps to Wright.)

WEST. You arrived sooner than I expected. But don't think for a moment that you can fool me as easily as you fooled the Queen and Candy. (*To Wright.*) So, you're the Lion ... HA! You're nothing but a cowardly principal! (*To Hansel.*) You're the Tin Man? In Candy's eyes, you were nothing but a little thin man ... (*To Gretel.*) And the Scarecrow ... are you prepared to get your stuffing knocked out ... Gretel!!!

DEWIE. No, O great majesty ... Don't do that ... Light him on fire. Just like you do it in your book.

HEWIE. Here's a torch. (*HE hands West a torch.*)

WEST. You don't fool me either, you despicable Decimals. My guards have spear points, not decimal points. And now you're all my prisoners. (*SHE shouts.*) Close castle doors. (*SHE waves her hand, and casts a spell to close the castle doors, as SHE laughs mercilessly. We hear the gates CLANG shut.*) You'd love for me to try and set this imitation straw man on fire, just like in my story. (*To Dorothy.*) So you could throw a bucket of water to put the flame out, dousing me instead. Causing me to melt. Well, I'm not afraid to do it. (*SHE taunts Gretel, the Scarecrow, with the torch.*) I live in a desert. There's no water here. I'm not afraid. Did anyone remember to bring any water? Hmmm?!!!?

(*THEY all look at each other stupefied.*)

WEST. Of course not. In your haste to save the world you forgot the most important thing ... water. And this is all thanks to you, my darling Beanie, and your beautiful book machine.

MR. WRIGHT. Your BAMBOOZLING Book Machine!

WEST. Call it what you want, I'm free! (*SHE laughs.*) I'm free! (*SHE laughs again.*) I'm FREE

LIBRUM. (*Suddenly appearing.*) But not for long. Take this! (*HE hurls a bucket of water at West.*)

WEST. WATER!

(*The water misses West. A chase into the audience begins. WEST runs into the audience, everyone following her. At one moment, there is another bucket of water thrown at her—this time the bucket is filled with confetti, à la Harlem Globetrotters—which falls on the children in the audience. The chase continues, ending onstage with DOROTHY throwing a third bucket of water which hits West, and SHE melts into the stage, [Note: original production used trap door in stage and "fog" effect.] leaving only her witch's hat behind.*)

WEST. (*As SHE is melting.*) AHHHH!!!! You cursed brat ... Look what you've done! I'm melting ... I'm melting. Oh what a world ... My world. Who would have thought a good little girl like you, could destroy my beautiful wickedness.

OHHHHHH!!!! Look out ... I'm melting ... I'm melting. (*WEST is gone. SMOKE fills the air.*)

    LIBRUM. Hail, Dorothy.

(*ALL start celebrating and shouting ad-libs as THEY gather around Dorothy and Librum.*)

    DOROTHY. We did it! We did it!
    GRETEL. It's all thanks to you, Professor.
    HANSEL. We live! We live!
    BEANIE. (*Still celebrating.*) But where's Snow White?

(*A silence falls over the group. The celebration ends as THEY remember that Snow White lies asleep back at the school without a prince to wake her.*)

    MR. WRIGHT. She's back at the school, still asleep.
    GRETEL. She sacrificed her life, so that we could live.
    HEWIE. I'll go back to Bookworld and force the prince to come back and kiss her.
    DEWIE. You'll never find him in time.
    DOROTHY. The least we can do is give her a proper funeral.
    LIBRUM. We'll take the space rider back to the auditorium.

(*ALL exit very slowly except for LIBRUM and BEANIE. As THEY talk in a special LIGHT, the scene is shifted back to the auditorium.*)

BEANIE. I wish I had never built that stupid machine.
LIBRUM. You're wrong, you were using your imagination. There's nothing wrong with that. Where do you think the world would be without young people using their imagination?
BEANIE. But we've lost Snow White ... And the world will be deprived of her story forever.
LIBRUM. Perhaps not, Beanie. There might be a way.

(*The LIGHTS come up on the auditorium. SNOW WHITE is still lying on the trophy table, asleep. The machine is also there. ALL enter as very sad MUSIC plays. When DOROTHY gets to SNOW WHITE the MUSIC fades.*)

DOROTHY. She was such a beautiful young woman.
GRETEL. (*To Librum.*) Can we take her back to Bookworld with us?
LIBRUM. Why? We have a prince amongst us. All he has to do is kiss her.
HANSEL. Who?
LIBRUM. Our pal, the Prince, Mr. Wright.

MR. WRIGHT. Me? I ... I ... I ... I'm not a prince, I'm a princiPAL. There's a difference you know.
GRETEL. You have to try it.

(*EVERYONE encourages Wright to do it. HE crosses over to give Snow White a kiss. As HE kisses her MUSIC swells, but never climaxes as she doesn't wake up. Depression once again falls over the group.*)

MR. WRIGHT. I tried.
DEWIE. (*To Librum.*) Shall I put her into the space rider?
LIBRUM. Yes.

(*DEWIE starts to pick up Snow White.*)

GRETEL. Let Hansel try!!
DEWIE. But he's not a prince!!
DOROTHY. Let him try ... We've got nothing to lose.

(*LIBRUM nods approval. EVERYONE encourages Hansel to kiss Snow White. HE walks to her. As HE kisses her MUSIC swells, but doesn't climax as Snow White doesn't wake up. Depression falls over the group once again.*)

DEWIE. Shall I take her?
LIBRUM. Put her in the space rider.

(*DEWIE starts to pick up Snow White.*)

DOROTHY. Wait!!! What are the qualifications that make a person a prince?
LIBRUM. They must be innocent and pure.
MR. WRIGHT. That's right!

(*ALL look at him.*)

MR. WRIGHT. I read it in a book ... When I was young!
HANSEL. But who among us is more innocent and pure than I?
DOROTHY. BEANIE!!!
BEANIE. But I've never kissed a girl before!
LIBRUM. Well, the time has come ...

(*EVERYONE now encourages Beanie to go forward and kiss Snow White. HE walks to her, the MUSIC swells, BEANIE can't do it. HE turns away embarrassed. All encourage him more. HE leans over and kisses Snow White. But the MUSIC doesn't climax as Snow doesn't wake up. Depression once again falls over the group. After a moment SNOW WHITE starts to stir. SHE wakes up, stands, embraces Beanie as SHE says:*)

SNOW WHITE. My prince has come at last!!

(The MUSIC finally climaxes. There is a moment of celebration, and then despair falls over ALL except WRIGHT and BEANIE.)

MR. WRIGHT. What's wrong? The witches are gone. Let's celebrate.
DEWIE. You don't understand. The witches might be gone, but without the witches ... these people don't have lives ... their lives only existed in books.
LOUIE. And without the witches, their books don't exist.
MR. WRIGHT. They can stay here and go to my school. We'll give them new lives as students.
LIBRUM. That's a nice thought, Mr. Wright, but unless we can remove the books from the machine, these characters have no future.
BEANIE. I can do that.
LIBRUM. You CAN??!! But the key is broken.
BEANIE. I have another key. Hidden in the machine.
LIBRUM. You do?
BEANIE. I would've said so earlier, but no one ever asked.
MR. WRIGHT. Then your stories can go back to normal, and you can live forever. Get the key, Beanie.

(BEANIE walks to the machine and takes a key from a secret compartment. HE inserts the key and turns the machine on. The MACHINE

starts to hum and spit and buzz. The LIGHTS start to flash. HE pulls the books from the machine.)

MR. WRIGHT. Look, the sun is shining again.
LIBRUM. That must mean the witches are alive and well and back in their books.
DOROTHY. Bring on that Wicked Witch of the West.
HANSEL. I'm ready for some juicy gingerbread.
GRETEL. Ja, der Bruder.
SNOW WHITE. (*To Beanie.*) Each time I am kissed, as a young reader reads my story ... I'll never be kissed by a prince as sweet as you, my Beanie.
LIBRUM. Decimals, prepare the space rider for the journey back to Bookworld.

(*DECIMALS salute and exit.*)

DOROTHY. (*To Beanie.*) I think I'll miss you most of all. (*SHE hugs Beanie and then exits.*)
HANSEL. (*Shaking Beanie's hand.*) Thank you, brave Beanie.
GRETEL. (*Hugging Beanie.*) Yes, thank you, brave Beanie.
HANSEL. Come, sister.
GRETEL. Ja, der Bruder.

(*THEY exit hand in hand.*)

SNOW WHITE. Goodbye, my Prince Charming. (*SHE hugs Beanie and then exits.*)
LIBRUM. (*Walks to Beanie.*) I hope you've learned your lesson with that Bamboozling Book Machine?
BEANIE. I don't even know what that means.
LIBRUM. Bamboozle. To mislead.

(*HE exits. The space rider takes off with much special EFFECTS and SOUND. BEANIE and WRIGHT wave goodbye. THEY are gone. BEANIE turns to Wright.*)

BEANIE. I'm sorry for bungling everything.
MR. WRIGHT. I'm proud of you, Beanie. You handled yourself well in a crisis situation. Let's go home.
BEANIE. In a second, Mr. Wright. (*HE picks up the three books off the machine.*) I want to read these books before I go ... to find out what REALLY happens to my new friends.

(*HE sits on the edge of the stage and begins to read, WRIGHT stands over him, a proud smile on his face, as the LIGHTS fade to black and the MUSIC swells.*)

The End

COSTUME PLOT

<u>MR WRIGHT</u>
Conservative grey suit
White shirt
Tie
Black wing tip shoes
[as Dwarf:]
Green blouse
Green pants
Green hat
Green shoes
[as Cowardly Lion:]
lion costume

<u>BEANIE BOREN</u>
Black pants
Argyle vest
White shirt
Bow tie
High-top tennis shoes
Beanie hat with propeller

<u>QUEEN</u>
Medieval gown and cape
Crown
[as Old Woman:]
Peasant dress
Apron
Mop hat

<u>CANDY</u>
Tattered sack dress
Cape

WEST
Black dress
Cape
Pointed hat

DOROTHY
Gingham dress
White pinafore
White knee socks
Mary Jane shoes
[as Dwarf:]
Green blouse
Green pants
Green hat
Green shoes

HANSEL
Brown Lederhosen
Orange shirt
Vest
[as Dwarf:]
Green blouse
Green pants
Green hat
Green shoes
[as Tin Man:]
Funnel hat
Silver lame suit

GRETEL
Green dirndl
[as Dwarf:]
Green pants
Green hat
Green shoes

[as Scarecrow:]
Plaid work shirt
Bib overalls
Straw hat

<u>LIBRUM</u>
Gold leotard and tights
Gold cape
BW emblem on chest
Red briefs

<u>SNOW WHITE</u>
Medieval peasant dress with high collared cape

<u>ALL THREE DECIMALS</u>
Gold lame jumpsuits
[as Dwarfs:]
Green blouse
Green pants
Green hat
Green shoes
[as palace guards:]
Long brown coats with fur collars
Russian fur hats

PROPERTY PLOT

<u>School Auditorium - Scene 1</u>
Two chairs - CS
Podium - L of C
Table - SL
Awards on table
The Book Machine - SR
Four books - On machine
Sheet - Covering machine
Key - On machine
Key - Hide in machine
Hand mirror - Queen
Fireballs - West

<u>A clearing in a forest - Scene 2</u>
Backpack - Beanie
Canteen - Beanie

<u>School Auditorium - Scene 3</u>
Yard stick - Mr. Wright
Communicator - Librum
Broom - Snow White from off L
Basket of Apples - Queen

<u>West's Castle - Scene 4</u>
Table - DL
Crystal Ball - On table
Spiked leash - Beanie
Hourglass - On table

Candy's Cottage - Scene 5
Oven - SL
House - CS
Rock - DR
Band-aid - Librum
Small pail - Librum

West's Castle - Scene 6
(Same as Scene 4)

West's Castle - Scene 7
Watch - Dorothy
Cage - at base of steps
Torch - Louie
One bucket - Librum
One bucket - Off SR filled w/confetti
One bucket - Off SL

School Auditorium - Scene 8
Same as 1 and 3

Awards Table

Podium

Chairs

Machine

School Auditorium
Scenes 1, 3, 8

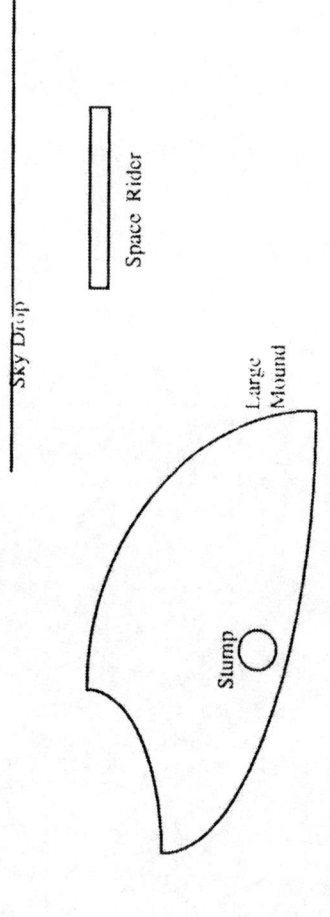

A Clearing in a Forest
Scene 2

Sky Drop

Oven

Table with hour glass

Above in one scene 4, 6

Gingerbread House

Rock

Rock

Rock

Candy's cottage
Scene 5

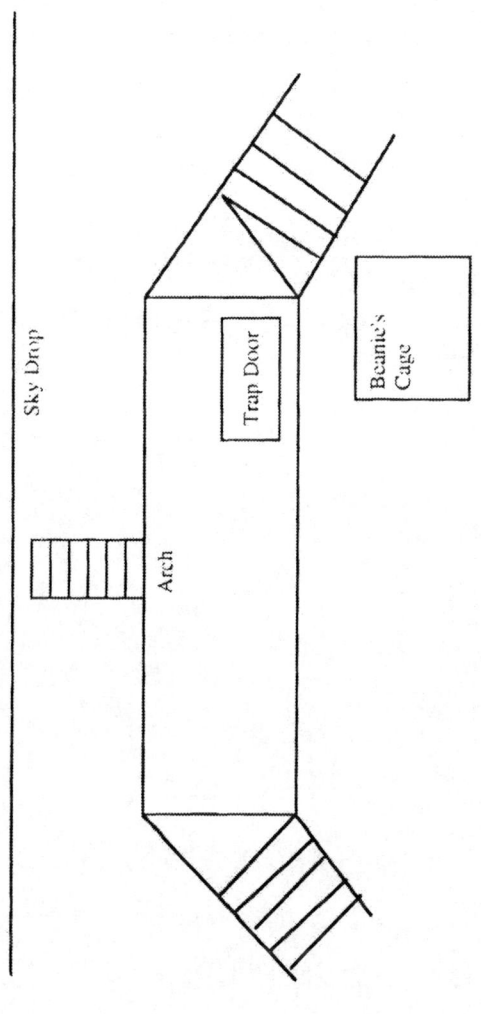

West's Castle
Scene 7

OTHER TITLES AVAILABLE FROM SAMUEL FRENCH

I STEP FROM A FAMOUS STORY
Clay Franklin

Monologues
Eighteen well-known tales are given a new look by having the main character from each tell a story. Poe, Hawthorne, Wilde, Twain, and O. Henry are some of the authors represented.

"They are a most useful anthology and come off remarkably well. The publication of this book fills a definite need."
– *Margaret Webster*

SAMUELFRENCH.COM

OTHER TITLES AVAILABLE FROM SAMUEL FRENCH

TREASURE ISLAND
Ken Ludwig

All Groups / Adventure / 10m, 1f (doubling) / Areas
Based on the masterful adventure novel by Robert Louis Stevenson, *Treasure Island* is a stunning yarn of piracy on the tropical seas. It begins at an inn on the Devon coast of England in 1775 and quickly becomes an unforgettable tale of treachery and mayhem featuring a host of legendary swashbucklers including the dangerous Billy Bones (played unforgettably in the movies by Lionel Barrymore), the sinister two-timing Israel Hands, the brassy woman pirate Anne Bonney, and the hideous form of evil incarnate, Blind Pew. At the center of it all are Jim Hawkins, a 14-year-old boy who longs for adventure, and the infamous Long John Silver, who is a complex study of good and evil, perhaps the most famous hero-villain of all time. Silver is an unscrupulous buccaneer-rogue whose greedy quest for gold, coupled with his affection for Jim, cannot help but win the heart of every soul who has ever longed for romance, treasure and adventure.

SAMUELFRENCH.COM

OTHER TITLES AVAILABLE FROM SAMUEL FRENCH

ENTER A FREE MAN
Tom Stoppard

Comedy / 5m, 3f / Combined Interior

Riley's a dreamer with all sorts of off-beat inventions, and his latest one is a double gummed envelope that can be used twice: once for sending and then turned inside out for replying. At home Riley is not well liked. His daughter is going to run away and marry a motorcyclist who turns out to be already married, and she can no longer support her dad in his unemployed habits. But this matters little to Riley, for he has this envelope deal, and also an indoor watering device for flowers. Trouble is, all his devices fall through including the indoor watering device when it is discovered you can't turn it off. And his dreams continue to burst in his face.

"A splendid full fledged comic creation."
– *London Observer*

SAMUELFRENCH.COM

OTHER TITLES AVAILABLE FROM SAMUEL FRENCH

TAKE HER, SHE'S MINE
Phoebe and Henry Ephron

Comedy / 11m, 6f / Various Sets

Art Carney and Phyllis Thaxter played the Broadway roles of parents of two typical American girls enroute to college. The story is based on the wild and wooly experiences the authors had with their daughters, Nora Ephron and Delia Ephron, themselves now well known writers. The phases of a girl's life are cause for enjoyment except to fearful fathers. Through the first two years, the authors tell us, college girls are frightfully sophisticated about all departments of human life. Then they pass into the "liberal" period of causes and humanitarianism, and some into the intellectual lethargy of beatniksville. Finally, they start to think seriously of their lives as grown ups. It's an experience in growing up, as much for the parents as for the girls.

"A warming comedy. A delightful play about parents vs kids. It's loaded with laughs. It's going to be a smash hit."
– *New York Mirror*

SAMUELFRENCH.COM